There are children who feel that
they're never alone . . .
. . . for wherever a mother's love goes,
there is home.

When God Himself would enter the world
to be known of man,
no door was Royal enough for his entrance,
save the doorway of Motherhood.

Mother O'Mine

A Mother's Treasury

Illustrated by Mary Engelbreit

**Andrews McMeel
Publishing**

Kansas City

www.andrewsmcmeel.com
www.maryengelbreit.com

is a registered trademark of Mary Engelbreit Enterprises, Inc.

00 01 02 03 MON 10 9 8 7 6 5 4 3 2

Library of Congress Cataloging-in-Publication Data

Engelbreit, Mary.
    Mother o'mine : a mother's treasury / illustrated by Mary Engelbreit.
        p. cm.
    ISBN 0-7407-1504-6
    1. Mothers--Literary collections. 2. Mothers--Quotations, maxims, etc. I. Title

PN6071.M7 E54 2000
808.8'03520431--dc21   00-061789

ATTENTION SCHOOL AND BUSINESSES
Andrews McMeel books are available at quantity discounts with bulk purchase for educational,
business, or sales promotional use. For information, please write to: Special Sales Department,
Andrews McMeel Publishing, 4520 Main Street, Kansas City, Missouri 64111.

Contents

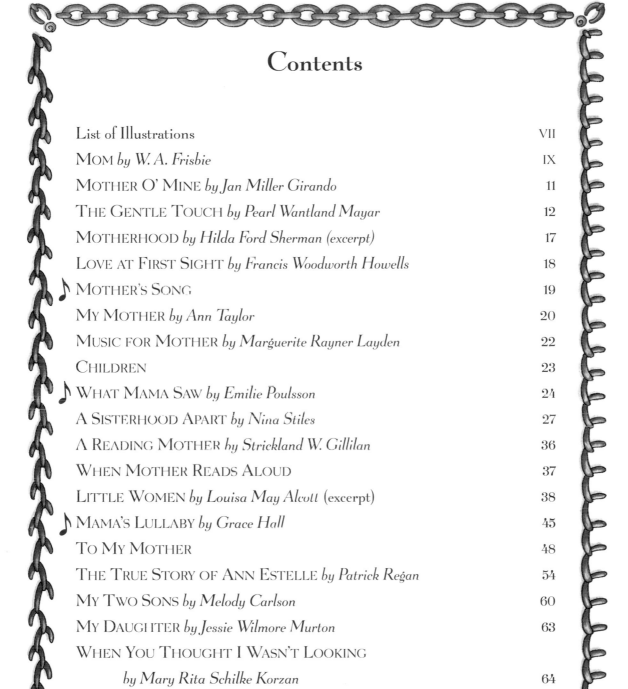

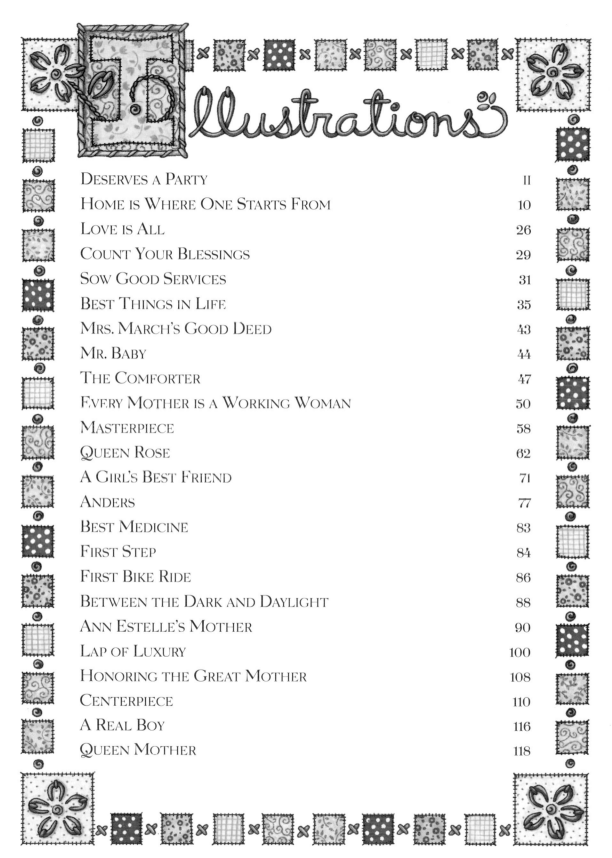

Illustrations

For my children
& my mother.

Romance fails us and so do friendships
but the relationship of Mother and Child
remains indelible and indestructible—
the strongest bond upon this earth.

—Theodor Reik

"MOM"

As Mother mine I honor you
  For all you did for me,
For tactfulness and patience, too,
  For dauntless loyalty;
Yet 'tis the things that may
    seem small
Which fondest thoughts impart;
"Mother" is on a pedestal
  But "Mom" is in my heart.
I honor "Mother" as I should,
  Serene and wise and calm;
As "Mother" you were kind and good
  But my real pal was "Mom."
To Mother mine I give my praise,
To her are thanks expressed
But all the time, through all
    my days,
  As "Mom" I love you best.
                    —W. A. Frisbie

HOME

IS WHERE ONE STARTS FROM

·T.S. ELIOT·····

Mother o' Mine

Jan Miller Girando

Where there is home, there's a mother who cares,
who gives comfort and kindness,
who listens and shares.

Where there is home, there's a mother who sees,
we need good times and laughter,
and sometimes a squeeze.

There's a mother who guides us whenever we're lost,
who gives of herself
without counting the cost,

A mother who's thoughtful and witty and wise,
who reflects all the love
in her little ones' eyes.

Where there is home, there are children who know,
that they may need a push,
if they're ever to grow.

There are children who feel that they're never alone,
for wherever a mother's love goes,
there is home.

The Gentle Touch
Pearl Wantland Mayar

The potter takes a lump of shapeless clay;
With skillful fingers and with practiced eyes,
He molds a thing of beauty and of worth
And smiles with satisfaction as it dries.

The artist blends his colors magically
To capture the elusive rainbow's hue,
To picture sunsets, mountains, trees, and sea
And feels his dreams of fame will all come true.

The singer's voice has power to thrill the soul,
To stir the heart to sadness and to tears,
With lullabies and hymns or dancing tunes—
With harmonies that linger through the years.

A mother takes a child with open mind
And guides, directs, and leads him through the strife
Of childhood, adolescence, youth, and love—
Her standards and ideals, his goal through life.

...It is not a slight thing
when they, who are so
fresh from God, love us.
—Dickens

Mother's arms are
made of tenderness,
and sweet sleep blesses
the child who lies therein.
—Victor Hugo

What does little baby weigh
    Laughing, merry, full of play?
To his mother I am told,
He is worth his weight in gold.

Not flesh of my flesh nor bone of my bone
    but still miraculously my own
Don't ever forget, even for one single minute,
    you didn't grow under my heart . . . but in it.

— Anonymous

God sends us children
for another purpose
than merely to keep up the race:
to enlarge our hearts; to make us unselfish,
and full of kindly sympathies and affections;
to give our souls higher aims,
and to call all our faculties
to extend enterprise and exertion;
to bring round our firesides bright faces,
and happy smiles,
and loving, tender hearts.

—Mary Howitt

Motherhood
Hilda Ford Sherman

When I first looked at baby's face
   I thought I heard the angels sing,
Their music seemed to flood the air,
   And in my heart it seemed to ring.

For a moment I was lifted
   Far above all earthly things;
And a grateful prayer I murmured
   For the joy a baby brings.

Love At First Sight

Francis Woodworth Howells

I met her in the hospital
    Just thirty years ago,
I met and loved her instantly
    And she loved me I know.

She, woman fashion, told her love,
    I must have seemed absurd,
So struck with all her loveliness,
    I couldn't say a word.

But we knew then, as we know now,
    We'll love till time is done.
For you see she was my mother,
    And I, her brand new son.

Mother's Song

(Traditional Nursery Song)
Author Unknown

There's not a rose where'er I seek
    As comely as my baby's cheek.
There's not a comb of honey-bee,
    So full of sweets as babe to me.
And it's O! sweet, sweet! and a lullaby.

There's not a star that shines on high,
    Is brighter than my baby's eye.
There's not a boat upon the sea,
    Can dance as baby does to me.
And it's O! sweet, sweet! and a lullaby.

No silk was ever spun so fine
    As is the hair of baby mine.
My baby smells more sweet to me
    Than smells in spring the elder tree.
And it's O! sweet, sweet! and a lullaby.

My Mother

Ann Taylor

Who fed me from her gentle breast
And hushed me in her arms to rest,
And on my cheek sweet kisses prest?
My mother.

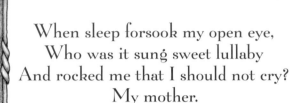

When sleep forsook my open eye,
Who was it sung sweet lullaby
And rocked me that I should not cry?
My mother.

Who sat and watched my infant head
When sleeping in my cradle bed,
And tears of sweet affection shed?
My mother.

When pain and sickness made me cry,
Who gazed upon my heavy eye
And wept, for fear that I should die?
My mother.

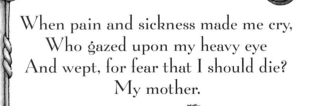

Who ran to help me when I fell
And would some pretty story tell,
Or kiss the part to make it well?
My mother.

Who taught my infant lips to pray,
To love God's holy word and day,
And walk in wisdom's pleasant way?
My mother.

And can I ever cease to be
Affectionate and kind to thee
Who wast so very kind to me,—
My mother.

Oh no, the thought I cannot bear;
And if God please my life to spare
I hope I shall reward thy care,
My mother.

When thou art feeble, old and gray,
My healthy arm shall be thy stay,
And I will soothe thy pains away,
My mother.

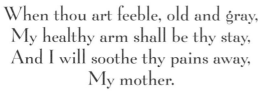

And when I see thee hang thy head,
'Twill be my turn to watch thy bed,
And tears of sweet affection shed,—
My mother.

Music for Mother

Marguerite Rayner Layden

Baby's hands are little and chubby,
Unskilled and fumbling, too,
But, oh my heart,
He plucks from your strings
Music far sweeter than others do.

Children

Children are what mothers are.

No fondest father's fondest care

Can fashion so the infant heart

As those creative beams that dart,

With all their hopes and fears, upon

The cradle of a sleeping son.

What Mama Saw

Written by: Emilie Poulsson
Music by: Eleanor Smith
Adapted by: Terry Kluytmans

What do you think
Mama saw on the hill?
Three little lambs
That were all lying still.
White woolly lambs
By the white woolly sheep.
All tuckered out,
They were going to sleep.

What do you think
Mama saw in the shed?
Two tiny colts
That were going to bed.
Quiet they kept,
Not a kick or a leap;
Frisking no more,
They were going to sleep.

Under the barn
Can you guess what she saw?
Curly-tailed pigs
Snuggled up in the straw.
Close by their mother
They lay in a heap
Squealing no more,
They were going to sleep.

What do you think
Mama sees while she sings?
Fairest and dearest
Of all little things!
Baby, my darling,
How quiet you keep,
Hearing of animals
Going to sleep.

Still as the curly-tailed
Pigs in a heap,
Still as the colts,
Not a kick or a leap,
Still as the lambs,
My beloved, you keep,
While Mama sings about
Going to sleep.

A Sisterhood Apart

Nina Stiles

I often think that had a mother been
The hostess there that evening at the inn,
There would have been no question of a stall.
She would have found some place within her hall
For Mary to lay down her tired head,
Perhaps she would have given her own bed.
And in the cradle of her own wee son,
She might have placed that night the Holy One;
Not with the thought of harboring a King,
Or any hope of gain her act might bring,
But from the simple goodness of her heart,
For mothers are a sisterhood apart.

In the sheltered simplicity
of the first days after a baby is born,
one sees again the magical closed circle.
The miraculous sense of two people
existing only for each other.
—Anne Morrow Lindbergh

There is no other closeness in human life
like the closeness between a mother and her baby;
chronologically, physically, and spiritually,
they are just a few heartbeats away
from being the same person.
—Susan Cheever

To her whose heart is my heart's quiet home,
To my first love, my Mother, on whose knee
I learnt love-lore that is not troublesome.
—Christina Rossetti

COUNT YOUR BLESSINGS

I shall never forget my mother,
for it was she who planted and nurtured
the first seeds of good within me.
She opened my heart to the impressions of nature;
she awakened my understanding
and extended my horizon,
and her precepts exerted an everlasting influence
upon the course of my life.

—Immanuel Kant

SOW GOOD SERVICES; SWEET REMEMBRANCES WILL GROW FROM THEM.

Mde. de Stael

ALL THAT I AM OR HOPE TO BE I OWE TO MY MOTHER

ABRAHAM ✳ LINCOLN

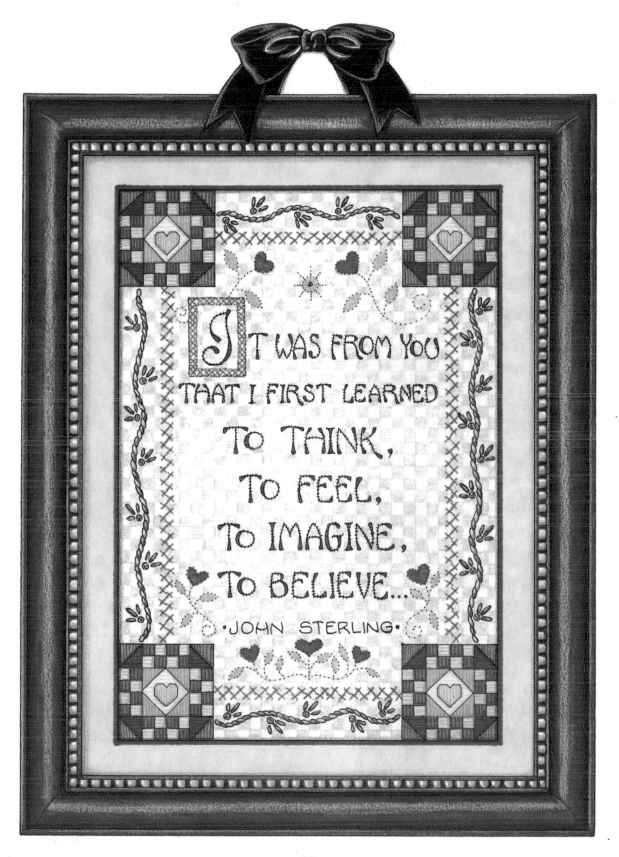

IT WAS FROM YOU
THAT I FIRST LEARNED

TO THINK,
TO FEEL,
TO IMAGINE,
TO BELIEVE...

·JOHN STERLING·

The real achievement of motherly love
lies not in the mother's love for the small infant,
but in her love for the growing child.
—Erich Fromm

My mother had a great deal
of trouble with me,
but I think she enjoyed it.
—Mark Twain

'TWAS I.

THE BEST THINGS IN LIFE... AREN'T THINGS!

A Reading Mother
Strickland W. Gillilan

I had a mother who read to me
Sagas of pirates who scoured the sea,
Cutlasses clenched in their yellow teeth,
"Blackbirds" stowed in the hold beneath.

I had a Mother who read me lays
Of ancient and gallant and golden days;
Stories of Marmion and Ivanhoe,
Which every boy has a right to know.

I had a Mother who read me the things
That wholesome life to the boy heart brings—
Stories that stir with an upward touch,
Oh, that each mother of boys were such!

You may have tangible wealth untold,
Caskets of jewels and coffers of gold.
Richer than I you can never be—
I had a Mother who read to me.

When Mother Reads Aloud

When mother reads aloud the past
Seems real as every day;
I hear the tram of armies vast,
I see the spears and lances cast,
I join the thrilling fray;
Brave knights and ladies fair and proud
I meet when mother reads aloud.

When mother reads aloud, far lands
Seem very near and true;
I cross the desert's gleaming sands,
Or hunt the jungle's prowling bands,
Or sail the ocean blue;
Far heights, whose peaks the cold mists shroud,
I scale, when mother reads aloud.

When mother reads aloud I long
For noble deeds to do—
To help the right, redress the wrong,
It seems so easy to be strong, so
    simple to be true,
O, thick and fast the visions crowd
When mother reads aloud.

Merry Christmas

From Little Women
Louisa May Alcott

Jo was the first to wake in the gray dawn of Christmas morning. No stockings hung at the fireplace, and for a moment she felt as much disappointed as she did long ago, when her little sock fell down because it was so crammed with goodies. Then she remembered her mother's promise, and slipping her hand under her pillow, drew out a crimson-covered book. She knew it very well, for it was the beautiful old story of the best life ever lived, and Jo felt that it was a true guidebook for any pilgrim going the long journey. She woke Meg with a "Merry Christmas," and bade her see what was under her pillow. A green-covered book appeared, with the same picture inside, and a few words written by her mother, which made their one present very precious in their eyes. Presently Beth and Amy woke, to rummage and find their little books also—one dove-colored, the other blue; and all sat looking at and talking about them, while the east grew rosy with the coming day.

In spite of small vanities, Margaret had a sweet and pious nature, which unconsciously influenced her sisters, especially Jo, who loved her very tenderly, and obeyed her because her advice was so gently given.

"Girls," said Meg seriously, looking from the tumbled head beside her to the two little nightcapped ones in the room beyond, "mother wants us to read and love and mind these books, and we must begin at once. We used to be faithful about it; but since father went away, and all this war trouble unsettled us, we have neglected many things. You can do as you please; but I shall keep my book on the table here, and read a little every morning as

soon as I wake, for I know it will do me good, and help me through the day."

Then she opened her new book and began to read. Jo put her arm around her, and, leaning cheek to cheek, read also, with a quiet expression so seldom seen on her restless face.

"How good Meg is! Come, Amy, let's do as they do. I'll help you with the hard words, and they'll explain the things we don't understand," whispered Beth, very much impressed by the pretty books and her sisters' example.

"I'm glad mine is blue," said Amy; and then the rooms were very still while the pages were softly turned, and the winter sunshine crept in to touch the bright heads and serious faces with a Christmas greeting.

"Where is mother?" asked Meg, as she and Jo ran down to thank her for their gifts, half an hour later.

"Goodness only knows. Some poor creeter come a-beggin', and your ma went straight off to see what was needed. There never was such a woman for givin' away vittles and drink, clothes and firin'," replied Hannah, who had lived with the family since Meg was born, and was considered by them all more as a friend than a servant.

"She will be back soon, I think; so fry your cakes, and have everything ready," said Meg, looking over the presents which were collected in a basket and kept under the sofa, ready to be produced at the proper time. "Why, where is Amy's bottle of cologne?" she added, as the little flask did not appear.

"She took it out a minute ago, and went off with it to put a ribbon on it, or some such notion," replied Jo, dancing about the room to take the first stiffness off the new army slippers.

"How nice my handkerchiefs look, don't they? Hanna washed and ironed them for me, and I marked them all myself," said Beth, looking proudly at the somewhat uneven letters which had cost her such labor.

"Bless the child! She's gone and put 'Mother' on them instead of 'M. March.' How funny!" cried Jo, taking up one.

"Isn't it right? I thought it was better to do it so, because Meg's

initials are 'M. M.,' and I don't want anyone to use these but Marmee," said Beth, looking troubled.

"It's all right, dear, and a very pretty idea—quite sensible, too, for no one can ever mistake now. It will please her very much, I know," said Meg, with a frown for Jo and a smile for Beth.

"There's mother. Hide the basket, quick!" cried Jo, as a door slammed, and steps sounded in the hall.

Amy came hastily in, and looked rather abashed when she saw her sisters all waiting for her.

"Where have you been, and what are you hiding behind you?" asked Meg, surprised to see, by her hood and cloak, that lazy Amy had been out so early.

"Don't laugh at me, Jo! I didn't mean anyone should know till the time came. I only meant to change the little bottle for a big one, and I gave all my money to get it, and I'm truly trying not to be selfish anymore."

As she spoke, Amy showed the handsome flask which replaced the cheap one; and looked so earnest and humble in her little effort to forget herself that Meg hugged her on the spot, and Jo pronounced her "a trump," while Beth ran to the window, and picked her finest rose to ornament the stately bottle.

"You see I felt ashamed of my present, after reading and talking about being good this morning, so I ran round the corner and changed it the minute I was up; and I'm *so* glad, for mine is the handsomest now."

Another bang of the street door sent the basket under the sofa, and the girls to the table, eager for breakfast.

"Merry Christmas, Marmee! Many of them! Thank you for our books; we read some, and mean to every day," they cried, in chorus.

"Merry Christmas, little daughters! I'm glad you began at once, and hope you will keep on. But I want to say one word before we sit down. Not far away from here lies a poor woman with a newborn baby. Six children are huddled into one bed to keep from freezing, for they have no fire. There is nothing to eat over there; and the oldest boy came to tell me they were suffering from hunger and cold. My girls, will you give them your breakfast as a Christmas present?"

They were unusually hungry, having waited nearly an hour, and for a minute no one spoke; only a minute, for Jo exclaimed impetuously:

"I'm so glad you came before we began!"

"May I go and help carry the things to the poor little children?" asked Beth eagerly.

"I shall take the cream and muffins," added Amy, heroically giving up the articles she most liked.

Meg was already covering the buckwheats, and piling the bread into one big plate.

"I thought you'd do it," said Mrs. March, smiling as if satisfied. "You shall all go and help me, and when we come back we will have bread and milk for breakfast, and make it up at dinnertime."

They were soon ready, and the procession set out. Fortunately it was early, and they went through back streets, so few people saw them, and no one laughed at the queer party.

A poor, bare, miserable room it was, with broken windows, no fire, ragged bedclothes, a sick mother, wailing baby, and a group of pale, hungry children cuddled under one old quilt, trying to keep warm.

How the big eyes stared and the blue lips smiled as the girls went in!

"Ach, mein Gott! It is good angels come to us!" said the poor woman, crying for joy.

"Funny angels in hoods and mittens," said Jo, and set them laughing.

In a few minutes, it really did seem as if kind spirits had been at work there. Hannah, who had carried wood, made a fire, and stopped up the

broken panes with old hats and her own cloak. Mrs. March gave the mother tea and gruel, and comforted her with promises of help, while she dressed the baby as tenderly as if it had been her own. The girls, in the meantime, spread the table, set the children round the fire, and fed them like so many hungry birds—laughing, talking, and trying to understand the funny broken English.

"Das ist gut!" "Die Engel-kinder!" cried the poor things, as they ate, and warmed their purple hands at the comfortable blaze.

The girls had never been called angel children before, and thought it very agreeable, especially Jo, who had been considered a "Sancho" ever since she was born. That was a very happy breakfast, though they didn't get any of it; and when they went away, leaving comfort behind, I think there were not in all the city four merrier people than the hungry little girls who gave away their breakfast and contented themselves with bread and milk on Christmas morning.

"That's loving our neighbor better than ourselves, and I like it," said Meg, as they set out their presents, while their mother was upstairs collecting clothes for the poor Hummels.

"She's coming! Strike up, Beth! Open the door, Amy! Three cheers for Marmee!" cried Jo, prancing about, while Meg went to conduct mother to the seat of honor.

Beth played her gayest march, Amy threw open the door, and Meg enacted escort with great dignity. Mrs. March was both surprised and touched; and smiled with her eyes full as she examined her presents, and read the little notes which accompanied them. The slippers went on at once, a new handkerchief was slipped into her pocket, well scented with Amy's cologne, the rose fastened in her bosom, and nice gloves were pronounced a "perfect fit."

There was a good deal of laughing and kissing and explaining, in the simple, loving fashion which makes these home festivals so pleasant at the time, so sweet to remember long afterward.

MRS. MARCH GAVE THE MOTHER TEA AND GRUEL... WHILE SHE DRESSED THE BABY AS TENDERLY AS IF IT HAD BEEN HER OWN.

Mama's Lullaby

Written by: Grace Hall
French Folk Song

Baby dear, Mama's here,
Watching o'er your slumber.
Dream, my child, until the dawn
Wakes the daisies on the lawn.

Dream you float in a boat,
Under starry heavens;
Dreams of brooks and singing birds,
Scented breezes, tender words.

Dream of all, great and small,
Things serene and lovely;
Fairies, lambs, and butterflies,
Sleepy clouds in summer skies.

Sleep all night, in my sight,
Though you're off in dreamland;
Then, tomorrow, with the sun,
Back to Mama, little one!

To her you'll always be
Just a youngster at her knee.
—Edgar Guest

To My Mother

You too, my mother, read my rhymes
For love of unforgotten times,
And you may chance to hear once more
The little feet along the floor.

To nourish children
and raise them against odds
is in any time, any place,
more valuable than to fix bolts in cars
or design nuclear weapons.
—Marilyn French

My mother is a woman
who speaks with her life
as much as with her tongue.
—Kesaya E. Noda

Some are kissing mothers
and some are scolding mothers,
but it is love just the same,
and most mothers kiss and scold together.
—Pearl S. Buck

A mother holds
her children's hands for a while,
their hearts forever.
—Anonymous

They are not long,
the days of construction paper
and gilded rigatoni!
That's why we save
those things so relentlessly,
why the sisterhood
of motherhood,
those of us who
can instantly make friends
with a stranger
by discussing colic
and orthodonture,
have as our coat of arms
a sheet of small handprints
executed in finger paint.
— Anna Quindlen

s a Working Woman.

By no amount of agile exercising
of a wistful imagination
could my mother have been called lenient.
Generous she was, indulgent, never.
Kind, yes; permissive, never.
In her world, people she accepted
paddled their own canoes,
pulled their own weight,
put their own shoulders
    to their own plows
        and pushed like hell.
                    —Maya Angelou

A mother is someone
who dreams great dreams for you
but then lets you
chase the dreams
you have for yourself
and loves you just the same.
—Anonymous

dream

The True Story of Ann Estelle

Patrick Regan

Any Mary Engelbreit fan worth her checks and cherries can identify Ann Estelle on sight. Her wide-brimmed hat, wire-rimmed spectacles and tell-it-like-it-is attitude have made her a recurring favorite in Mary's art.

But did you know there was a *true* story behind this prim and proper (but peppery) little girl?

The *original* Ann Estelle, Ann Estelle Devine, was born in 1902 in St. Louis, Missouri. And she too was proper, principled, and loved by many—including her granddaughter, Mary Engelbreit.

"I loved just being with Ann Estelle," Mary says enthusiastically when asked about her grandmother. "She and the two sisters (Mary's mother and aunt) were all so wonderful, and they were very funny together." Mary has fond memories of visiting her grandmother's tidy house as a child. "She had such great things in her china cabinet, and she would let me take them out and look at them," she continues. "She liked it that I liked that kind of stuff."

Mary is certainly not alone in her warm memories of—and affection for—her grandmother. "Everybody loved her," recalls Mary's mother, Mary Lois Engelbreit, one of Ann Estelle's two daughters. "Well, she was easy to love," chimes in Mary's aunt Audy, finishing the thought in true sisterly fashion.

The two sisters took a few hours to reminisce about their mother on a mild spring day in the St. Louis-area home of Mary Lois—not far from where they and a brother were raised by Ann Estelle and their father, Leonard Stedeline.

Both sisters endearingly remember their mother as a woman of grace, beauty, and style. "She was the pick of the lot," says Audy matter-of-factly. Her sister continues, "She was a pretty lady and she dressed nicely. She had a good sense of humor, and she and daddy liked to go out and have fun."

Her mode of dress, like that of her often sailor-suited namesake, was an identifying trait of Ann Estelle. "She was always very tailored," remembers Mary Lois. "And she dressed us well, too. On Saturdays we'd put on the hats and the gloves and get on the bus downtown to shop and have lunch." Then, laughing, she adds, "Mother used to say, 'You might as well be dead as out of style.'"

That little gem is just one of the many "pearls of wisdom" that Ann Estelle shared with her daughters. To this day, the girls can recite from memory the four-point advice their mother passed along to each of them before they married: Never go out looking like a slob; when you get married, don't give up your own friends; if you have an argument with your husband, keep it to yourself (other people will remember it long after you've forgotten what it was about); when you're raising your children always remember when you were a child yourself.

And while they're quick to point out that their mother was "a conscientious wife and mother," they also admit that she wasn't afraid to buck convention—another trait that the illustrated Ann Estelle would find familiar. "Mother was one of very few women who drove her own car back in those days," remembers Mary Lois. She was forever picking up other people to go play bridge or go shopping or whatever. She was on the go a lot."

Much of her driving involved ministering to the needs of the less fortunate. She regularly ferried the nuns of the Little Helpers of the Holy Souls on their appointed rounds to visit the poor. And in her later years she ran a residence home for working women.

Ann Estelle was an individualist and an independent thinker — a matriarch with a strength of character that she passed along to two subsequent generations of strong women… and even to the fictional character that bears her name.

In truth, the plucky Ann Estelle character, the deliverer of such memorable lines as "Snap out of it!" and "We don't care how they do it in New York," more closely reflects her creator, Mary Engelbreit, than her namesake. By her daughter's account, Ann Estelle Devine was a woman who stayed in control of her emotions. "The worst thing she'd ever say was "Hell's bells," Mary Lois remembers. And while Ann Estelle didn't share her granddaughter's artistic sensibilities, she did have some colorful ways of expressing herself. "If she was really annoyed at something, she'd say, 'I'm going to walk until my hat floats,'" remembers Mary Lois, explaining the allusion to the nearby Mississippi River.

Ann Estelle was proper to a fault, and poor grammar was something that she simply would not suffer. Both daughters recall frequent grammatical "refreshers." "'You don't *make* chicken,' she'd say, 'You *cook* chicken.'" Audy smiles, relating some of her mother's constructive admonitions. "'You don't *make* dinner. You *prepare* dinner.'" And Mary Lois can't resist joining in. "If we'd say, 'I'm done.' She'd say, '*Cakes* are done. You're not done. You're *finished*.'" "She took great pride in us," Mary Lois continues. "She cared about raising us properly, and that made us feel good. We knew we were loved." Audy uses another Ann Estelle*ism*… to reinforce her sister's words: "If we'd make a mistake and try to shrug it off, mother would say, 'What the bird does in his cage, he does out.'"

Although Mary Engelbreit's illustrated Ann Estelle does share her namesake's knack for creative expression, Mary admits that she wasn't trying to capture her grandmother's personality with the spunky character she created. Her motivation for naming 'Ann Estelle' was much simpler. "I thought it was such a *different* name," she says. "And I wanted a name that meant something to me—not just some made-up name." Then, with a smile, she adds, "Also, I knew it would make my mom happy."

Mary's mother *is* clearly tickled by the name—and pleased with the link it provides to three generations of women. "The funny thing is," Mary Lois says, "Mary didn't even call her grandmother Ann Estelle—and she didn't hear too many other people call her that either. Most friends just called her "Ann."

Such a revelation might come as a surprise to the Mary Engelbreit faithful, but Mary confirms its truth. "When I was a kid I had trouble pronouncing 'Ann Estelle'," Mary explains. "It came out, 'Datel,' and for some reason that just stuck. And because I was the oldest grandchild, that's what all the other grandchildren called her, too."

Ann Estelle didn't live to see the birth of the character that bears her name, yet Mary Lois says she often thinks about how her mother would react to having a character named after her. "I think she'd get a big kick out of it," she says. "She'd love it. That little girl's name is a nice tribute to a lady who was loved by a lot of people."

MARY LOIS, ANN ESTELLE, AUDY, 1929, . . . A MOTHER OF GRACE AND STYLE.

Our mothers and grandmothers have,
more often than not,
anonymously handed on the creative spark,
the seed of the flower
they themselves never hoped to see—
like a sealed letter
they could not plainly read.

—Alice Walker

My Two Sons
Melody Carlson

My two sons,
I always wanted you.
Even when I was a little girl
Playing with baby dolls.
I clothed them and fed them,
Rocked them and sang a lullaby.
Thinking that one day,
I would have babes of my own.

And God gave me you,
My two sons.
And I clothed you and fed you,
I rocked you to sleep
And sang you a lullaby.
And it was wonderful.
I wanted it to last
Forever.

But quickly you grew older,
With sturdy legs and grinning faces.
And we made a sandbox,
Played with Legos.
And read stories.
We learned to ride bikes
And mended owies.
And you grew up.

Now you are young men.
Both over six feet tall,
    with whiskers.
It feels like you don't
    need me—very much.

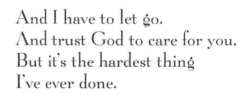

And I have to let go.
And trust God to care for you,
But it's the hardest thing
I've ever done.

My two sons,
I always wanted you.
But now all I can do
Is watch and pray,
That you will let God
Clothe you, and feed you,
Rock you and sing
    you a lullaby.
And it will be wonderful.

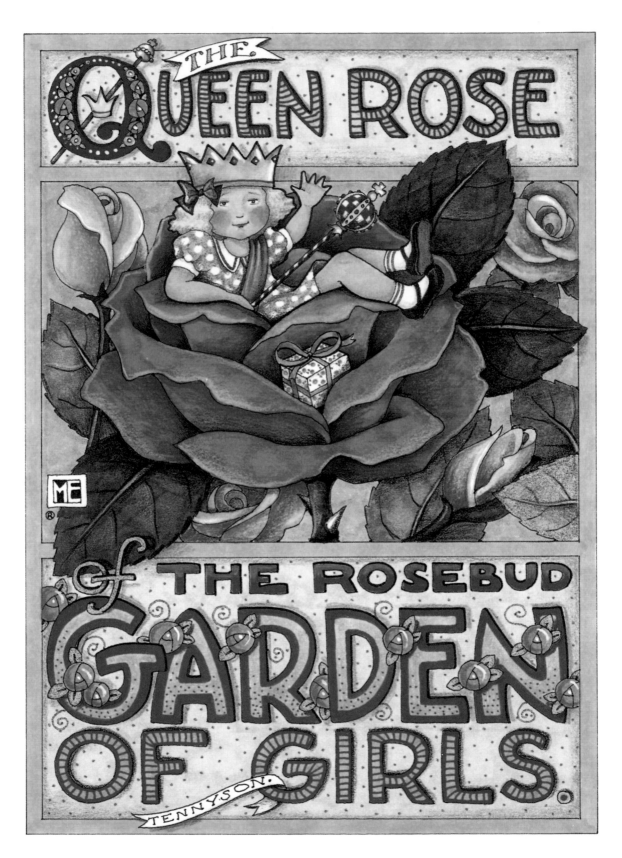

My Daughter
Jessie Wilmore Murton

God gave to me a little flower
To tend with loving care,
And never earthly garden held
A blossom half so fair!
Her smiling eyes, my stars, my skies,
Her laughter, rippling water!
Her joy, her woe, mine doubly so—
Flesh of my flesh, my daughter!

God gave to me a little flower!
And yet, not mine alone—
Someday He will require of me
The blossom, fully grown!
Her smiling eyes, my stars, my skies,
Her laughter, rippling water!
Her joy, her woe, mine doubly so—
Heart of my heart, my daughter!

When You Thought I Wasn't Looking

Mary Rita Schilke Korzan

When you thought I wasn't looking
You hung my first painting on the refrigerator
And I wanted to paint another.

When you thought I wasn't looking
You fed a stray cat
And I thought it was good to be kind to animals.

When you thought I wasn't looking
You baked a birthday cake just for me
And I knew that little things were special things.

When you thought I wasn't looking
You said a prayer
And I believed there was a God
that I could always talk to.

When you thought I wasn't looking
You kissed me good-night
And I felt loved.

When you thought I wasn't looking
I saw tears come from your eyes
And I learned that sometimes things hurt—
But that it's alright to cry.

When you thought I wasn't looking
You smiled
And it made me want to look that pretty too.

When you thought I wasn't looking,
You cared
And I wanted to be everything I could be.

When you thought I wasn't looking—
I looked...
And wanted to say thanks
For all those things you did
When you thought I wasn't looking.

Home Influences

There is music in the word home.
To the old it brings a bewitching strain
from the harp of memory;
to the young it is a reminder
of all that is near and dear to them.
Among the many songs we are wont to listen to,
there is not one more cherished
than the touching melody
of "Home, Sweet, Home."

The Old Arm Chair

Eliza Cook

I love it! I love it!
And who shall dare
To chide me for loving that old arm-chair?
I've treasured it long as a sainted prize;
I've bedewed it with tears and emblamed it with sighs
'Tis bound by a thousand bands to my heart;
Not a tie will break, not a link will start.
Would you learn the spell?
A mother sat there;
And a sacred thing is that old arm-chair.

She is clothed with strength and dignity;

she can laugh at the days to come.

She speaks with wisdom,

and faithful instruction is on her tongue.

She watches over the affairs of her household

and does not eat the bread of idleness.

Her children arise and call her blessed;

her husband also, and he praises her:

"Many women do noble things,

but you surpass them all."

—Proverbs 31:25-29

M-O-T-H-E-R

By Howard Johnson

"M" is for the million things she gave me,

"O" means only that she's growing old,

"T" is for the tears she shed to save me,

"H" is for her heart of purest gold;

"E" is for her eyes, with love-light shining,

"R" means right, and right she'll always be,

Put them all together, they spell "MOTHER,"

A word that means the world to me.

A Pinch of This and a Pinch of That

When mother used to mix a dough
Or make a batter long ago,
When I was only table high
I used to like to just stand by
And watch her for a little while,
She'd sing a little and maybe smile,
And talk to me and tell me—what?
Well! Things I never have forgot.

70

I'd ask her how to make a cake—
First she'd say, some sugar take,
Then some flour, an egg or two,
Then put in—to make it good—
(This part I never understood
And often used to wonder at)
A pinch of this and a pinch of that.

Then she'd say, "My little girl,
When you've grown up and childhood's done,
And maybe Mother is far away,
Just remember what I say.
For life's a whole lot like a cake,
Yes, life's a thing we have to make
Much like a cake or pie or bread,
You'll find, my little girl," my Mother said.

I didn't understand her then,
But now her words come back again.
Before my eyes, the past appears—
A life of laughter and of fears,
And both the bitter, and the sweet
Have made that life of mine complete.

The things I have and the things I miss
Are a pinch of that and a pinch of this
But now, I think I know the way
To make a life as she would say;
Put in the wealth to serve your needs,
But don't leave out the lovely deeds.
Put on the great things you mean to do,
But don't leave out the good, the true.
Put in, wherever you are at,
A pinch of this and a pinch of that.

The Watcher

Margaret Widdemer

She always leaned to watch for us,
　　Anxious if we were late,
In winter by the window,
　　In summer by the gate;

And though we mocked her tenderly,
　　Who had such foolish care,
The long way home would seem more safe
　　Because she waited there.

Her thoughts were all so full of us,
　　She never could forget!
And so I think that where she is
　　She must be watching yet,

Waiting till we come home to her,
　　Anxious if we are late—
Watching from Heaven's window,
　　Leaning from Heaven's gate.

Wonderful Mother
Pat O'Reilly

God made a wonderful mother,
A mother who never grows old;
He made her smile of the sunshine,
And He moulded her heart of pure gold,
In her eyes He placed bright shining stars,
In her cheeks fair roses you see;
God made a wonderful mother,
And he gave that dear mother to me.

The Cap that Mother Made

A Swedish Tale

Once upon a time there was a little boy, named Anders, and he had a new cap. A prettier cap was never seen, for his mother herself had knit it; and who could ever make anything half so nice as Mother! The cap was red, except for a small part in the middle. That was green, for there had not been enough red yarn to make it all; and the tassel was blue.

Anders' brothers and sisters walked about admiring him; then he put his hands in his pockets and went out for a walk, for he was altogether willing that everyone should see how fine his mother had made him.

The first person he met was a farmhand walking beside a cart loaded with peat, and bidding his horse gee-up. When he saw Anders' new cap, the farmhand made a bow so deep that he bent nearly double, but Anders trotted proudly past him, holding his head very high.

At the turn of the road he came upon Lars, the tanner's boy. Lars was such a big boy that he wore high boots and carried a jack-knife. But oh, when he saw that cap, he stood quite still to gaze at it, and he could not help but going up close to Anders and fingering the splendid blue tassel.

"I'll give you my cap for yours," he cried, "and my jack-knife besides!"

ANDERS

Now this knife was a splendid one, and Anders knew that as soon as one has a jack-knife, one is almost a man. But still he would not for all the world give up, for the knife, the cap which Mother had made.

"Oh, no, I could not do that," he said. And then he nodded good-bye to Lars, and went on.

Soon after this Anders met a queer little lady. She curtsied to him until her skirts spread out like a balloon and she said: "Lad, you are so fine, why do you not go to the king's ball?"

"Yes, why do I not?" thought Anders. "With this cap, I am altogether fit to visit the king."

And off he went.

In the palace yard stood two soldiers with guns over their shoulders and shining helmets on their heads. When Anders went to pass them, they both leveled their guns at him.

"Where are you going, boy?" asked one of the soldiers.

"I am going to the king's ball," answered Anders.

"No, you are not," said the other soldier, trying to push him back. "Nobody can go to the king's ball without a uniform."

But just at this moment the princess came tripping across the yard, dressed in a white satin gown, with ribbons of gold.

"This lad has no uniform, it's true," she said, "but he has a very fine cap and that will do just as well. He shall come to the ball."

So she took Anders by the hand and walked with him up the broad marble stairs, past the soldiers who stood on every third step, through magnificent halls where gentlemen and ladies in silk and velvet were waiting about. And wherever Anders went, all the people bowed to him, for, as like as not, they thought him a prince when

they saw what it was that he wore on his head.

At the farther end of the largest hall a table was set with long rows of golden plates and goblets. On huge silver platters were piles of tarts and cakes. The princess sat down under a blue canopy with bouquets of roses on it; and she bade Anders to sit in a golden chair by her side.

"But you must not eat with your cap on your head," she said, and she started to take it off.

"Oh, yes, I can eat just as well with it on," said Anders, and he held on to it with both his hands, for if it were taken away from him, he did not feel sure he would ever get it again.

"Well, well, give it to me," begged the princess, "and I will give you a kiss."

The princess was beautiful, and Anders would surely have liked to be kissed by her, but not for anything in this world would he give up the cap that Mother had made. He only shook his head.

Then the princess filled his pockets full of cakes; she put her own heavy gold chain around his neck, and bent down and kissed him.

"Now will you give me the cap?" she said.

Anders moved farther back in his chair, but he never once took his hands from his head.

Then the doors were thrown open and the king himself entered, accompanied by gentlemen in glittering uniforms and plumed hats. The king wore a mantle of blue velvet, bordered with ermine, and he had a large gold crown on his head.

When he saw Anders in the golden chair, he smiled.

"That is a very fine cap that you have," he said.

"So it is," said Anders, "it is made of Mother's best yarn, and she has knit it herself, and everyone wants to get it away from me."

"But surely you would like to change caps with me," said the king, and he lifted his shining gold crown from his head.

Anders said never a word but when the king came nearer to him with his gold crown in one hand and the other hand outstretched toward that beautiful cap, then, with one jump, Anders was out of his chair. Like an arrow he darted out of the hall, through the palace, down the stairs, and across the yard. He ran so fast that the necklace the princess had given him fell from his neck, and all the cakes rolled out of his pockets.

But he had his cap! He had his cap! He had his cap! With both hands he clutched it tight as he ran back home to his mother's cottage.

"Well, Anders, where have you been?" cried his mother. So he told her all about what happened.

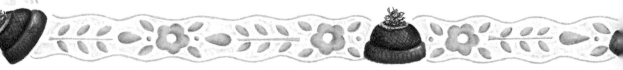

All his brothers and sisters stood around and listened with mouths wide open.

But when his big brother heard how he had refused to give his cap in exchange for the king's golden crown, he cried out:

"Anders, you were foolish! Just think of all the things you might have bought with the king's gold crown! Velvet jackets and long leather boots and silken hose, a sword. Besides, you could have bought yourself a much finer cap with a feather in it."

Anders' face grew red, very red. "I was not foolish," he answered sturdily, "I could never have bought a finer cap, not for all the king's crown. I could never have bought anything in all this world half so fine as the cap my mother made me!"

Then his mother took him up on her lap, and kissed him.

mother keeps a vigil at the bedside of her sick child.
The world calls it "fatigue," but she calls it love.
—Bishop Fulton J. Sheen

Mothers never change, I guess,
In their tender thoughtfulness.
All her gentle long life through
She is bent on nursing you.
—Edgar Guest

Most of all the other
beautiful things in life
come by twos and threes,
by dozens and hundreds.
Plenty of roses, stars,
sunsets, rainbows . . .
but only one mother
in the whole world.
—Kate Douglas Wiggins

A Mother Is...

Someone who cares when others care less.

Someone who encourages when others ridicule.

Someone who defends when others condemn.

Someone with patience when others are impatient.

Someone who appreciates when others fail to notice.

Someone who gives security in a world of insecurity.

Someone who is accepting when others reject.

A Mother is a friend for all time, to cherish and protect,

as her achievements will linger for generations.

Between the dark and daylight,
When the night is beginning to lower,
Comes a pause in the day's occupations,
That is known as the Children's Hour.

·LONGFELLOW·

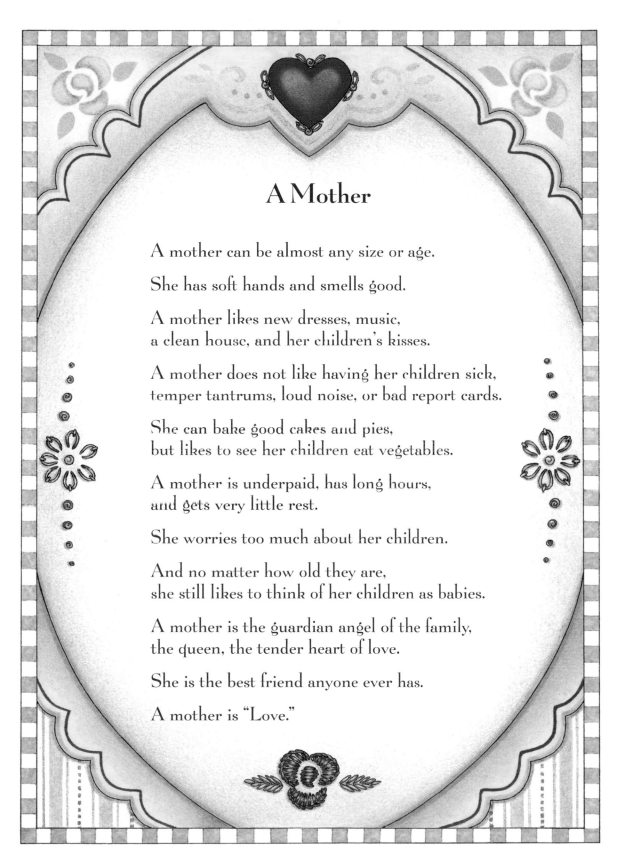

A Mother

A mother can be almost any size or age.

She has soft hands and smells good.

A mother likes new dresses, music,
a clean house, and her children's kisses.

A mother does not like having her children sick,
temper tantrums, loud noise, or bad report cards.

She can bake good cakes and pies,
but likes to see her children eat vegetables.

A mother is underpaid, has long hours,
and gets very little rest.

She worries too much about her children.

And no matter how old they are,
she still likes to think of her children as babies.

A mother is the guardian angel of the family,
the queen, the tender heart of love.

She is the best friend anyone ever has.

A mother is "Love."

O God, since ever I could speak,
My voice had fallen on faithful ears,
'Twas "Mother" in triumph hour,
And "Mother" in my time of tears.
— Laura C. Redden in "Dear Mother"

What Do Mothers Do all Day?

Marshall H. Hart

Every minute, to and fro,
     That's the way my hours go;
Bring me this, and take me that,
     Feed the dog, take out the cat.
Standing up I eat my toast,
     Drink my coffee, thaw the roast;
Empty the garbage, make the bed,
     Rush to church, then wash my head.
Sweep the kitchen, wax the floor,
     Scrub the woodwork, clean the doors;

Scour the bathtub, then myself,
     Vacuum carpets, straighten shelves.
Eat my sandwich on the run,
     Now my afternoon's begun;
To the baseball game I go,
     When will there be time to sew?
Meet the teacher, stop the fight,
     See the dentist, fly the kite;
Help with homework, do the wash,
     Iron the clothes, put on the squash.

Shop for groceries, cash a check,
　　Fight the crowds, now I'm a wreck!
Dinner time it soon will be,
　　"What's for dinner?" they ask,
Wait and see.
　　Dirty dishes crowd the sink,
Next there's popcorn, then a drink;
　　Will they never go to bed . . .
Will I ever get ahead?
　　"Bring me water," . . . "Get the light,"
Turn off the TV, lock the bike;
　　"Where's my pillow?' . . . "Hear my prayers,"
"Did you lock the door downstairs?"
　　At last in bed, my spouse and I,
Too tired to move, to weak to cry;
　　But as I doze I hear him say,
"What do mothers do all day?"

Where Does Mom Keep her Memories?

Where does Mom keep her memories?
In a box worn beyond repair,
Tucked inside are memories,
Ask and she will gladly share.

Tattered Valentines "To Mommy With Love,"
Papers boasting "Good Work ... Well Done!"
A hand print small and fragile,
Blue ribbons proudly won.

Macaroni shells that once formed a flower,
A baby picture smudged with kisses,
The first tooth the Fairy spared,
Cards of IOU's and loving wishes.

Where does Mom keep her memories?
In a box this precious cargo rests
Reminiscent of days long past,
The box of love is her treasure chest.

My Mother

She was as good as goodness is,
Her acts and all her words were kind,
And high above all memories
I hold the beauty of her mind.

—Frederic Hentz Adams

Measuring Rods

I know what mother's face is like,
Though it I cannot see:
It's like the music of a bell,
It's like the way the roses smell,
It's like the stories fairies tell—
It's all of these to me.

If we make our children happy now, we will make
Them happy twenty years hence by their memory of it.
Thus for all their lives do we link ourselves to
Those we love.

—Maggie B. Stewart

That Wonderful Mother of Mine

Clyde Hager

The moon never beams without bringing me dreams
    Of that wonderful mother of mine.
The birds never sing but a message they bring
    Of that wonderful mother of mine.
Just to bring back the time, that was so sweet to me,
    Just to bring back the days, when I sat on her knee.

I pray ev'ry night to our Father above,
    For that wonderful mother of mine.
I ask Him to keep her as long as He can
    That—wonderful mother of mine.
There are treasures on earth, that make life seem worthwhile,
    But there's none can compare to my mother's smile.

You are a wonderful mother, dear old Mother of mine.
    You'll hold a spot down deep in my heart,
'Till the stars no longer shine.
    Your soul shall live on forever,
On through the fields of time.
    For there'll never be another to me,
Like that wonderful Mother of mine.

Baby Shoes

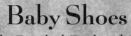

Isla Paschal Richardson

Two worn little shoes with a hole in the toe!
And why have I saved them? Well—all mothers know
There's nothing so sweet as a baby's worn shoe
And patter of little steps following you.

The feet they once held have grown slender and strong;
Tonight they'll be tired after dancing so long . . .
I guided her feet when she wore such as these . . .
Dear God, may I ask, won't You guide them now, please?

Light of Home

My son, thou wilt dream the world is fair,
And thou spirit will sigh to roam,
And thou must go; but never, when there,
Forget the light of home!
　　　　　　　　—Sarah Josepha Hale

THE LAP of LUXURY

Mother, Now I Understand

Virginia Jackson Safford

I thought I loved you, mother mine,
   As well as daughter could.
I took your sacrifices and
   I thought I understood
The love you had for me, that made
   Slaves of your willing hands—
But oh, the blind conceit of youth
   That thinks it understands!

There came to me, in joy, in pain,
   The gift of motherhood.
Ah then, oh mother, mother mine,
   I knew I understood
The willing toil, the joy, the fear,
   In that sweet heart of you—
Things no daughter can understand
   Till she's a mother, too!

Round the idea of one's mother,
the mind of man clings with fond affection.
It is the first thought stamped in our infant hearts,
when yet soft and capable to receiving
the most profound impressions,
and all the after feelings of the world
are more or less light in comparison.
I do not know that even in our old age
we do not look back to that feeling as
the sweetest we have ever known through life.
—Charles Dickens

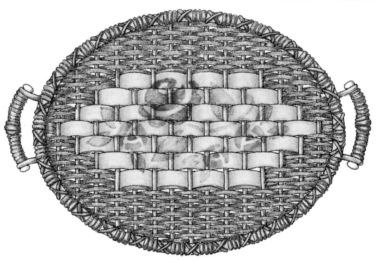

A picture memory brings to me;
I look across the years and see
Myself beside my mother's knee.
I feel her gentle hand restrain
My selfish moods, and know again
A child's blind sense of wrong and pain.
But wiser now, a man gray grown,
My childhood's needs are better known.
My mother's chastening love I own.
—John Greenleaf Whittier

A mother's love
is indeed the golden link that
Binds youth to age;
and he is still but a child,
However time may have furrowed his cheek,
Or silvered his brow,
who can yet recall with a
Softened heart, the fond devotion, or the gentle
Chidings, of the best friend that God ever gave us.
—Bovee

My Mother's Quilt
Rachel Van Crème

My Mother had a lovely quilt she treasured through the years;
It told her many a tender tale of bygone joys and tears.

A square of bright red calico
Her fingers would explore;
She wore it her first day at school,
She told me o'er and o'er!

To a narrow strip of yellowed white
Her eyes would often stray;
She wore that when a blushing bride,
Upon her Wedding Day.

That tiny piece of pink and whit
And then the tears would start;
Her first born in her arms was l
Close to her mother heart.

Her fingers touched a dainty blue
In reverence, lingered there;
"The little girl God needed," and
Her lips would move in prayer.

There, woven in my Mother's quilt
Was the record of her life;
The gray days and the golden ones,
Her years of joy and strife.

And when she left her earthly home
To cross that silent sea,
Her presence lingered, bright and warm
In this quilt she left with me.

But a mother's love endures through all:
in good repute, in bad repute,
in the face of the world's condemnation,
a mother still loves on, and still hopes . . .
still she remembers the infant smiles
that once filled her bosom with rapture,
the merry laugh,
the joyful soul of this childhood,
the opening promise of his youth,
and she can never be brought to think him all unworthy.
—Washington Irving

There was never a woman like her.
She was gentle as a dove
and brave as a lioness.
The memory of my mother
and her teachings were, after all,
the only capital I had to start life with,
and on that capital I have made my way.
—Andrew Jackson

My mother was the making of me.
She was so true and so sure of me.
I felt that I had someone to live for—
someone I must not disappoint.
The memory of my mother will always
be a blessing to me.
—Thomas Edison

COUNT YOUR
BLESSINGS

Honoring the Great Mother

From Simple Abundance
Sarah Ban Breathnach

*Mothering myself has become
a way of listening to my deepest needs,
and of responding to them
while I respond to my inner child.*

—Melinda Burns

Many women I know share a seldom-expressed yearning to be comforted. To be mothered. This voracious need is deep, palpable—and often unrequited. Instead, we are the ones who usually provide comfort, caught between the pressing needs of our children, our elderly parents, our partners, our friends, even our colleagues.

Though we are grown, we never outgrow the need for someone special to hold us, stroke our hair, tuck us into bed, and reassure us that tomorrow all will be well. Perhaps we need to reacquaint ourselves consciously with the maternal and deeply comforting dimension of Divinity in order to learn how to mother ourselves. The best way to start is to create—as an act of worship—a comfortable home that protects, nurtures, and sustains all who seek refuge within its walls.

I remember the flowers my Mother loved
And it seems I love the same,
As I wander often about my lawn,
Calling my flowers by name.

Just as she used to wander about
Gathering bright bouquets,
I find myself doing the same
Throughout the summer's day.

I like to take an old-fashioned vase,
Just as she used to do
And make up a mass arrangement
For beauty and fragrance, too.

The flowers she had in her garden
Are the flowers I have in mine
Sweet-peas, poppies and iris,
Verbena and columbine.

These were the ones she cherished the most,
And these are the ones I adore,
Even though I have many others,
Just as she had many more.

So on this day of remembrance
I'll arrange an old fashioned bouquet
Of beautiful flowers from the garden
For a tribute to "Mother's Day."

Ideals of Life

You may talk of fashion's leader—
Paint her finer than a queen,
And try to make our lowly lot
And lowly living mean;
But I tell you, sir, the fairest
And the best thing that I have seen,

Were common men and women,
Used to humble work and ways;
Doing what was right and honest
Without favor, without praise,
Lighting up the night behind them
With the whiteness of their days.

There is one that shines upon me
From the mists of memory—
A woman, with the weakness
Of a woman, it may be;—
And naught to me are social queens
While on earth holds such as she!

Her homespun sleeve is more to me
Than all your bordered trains;
For in the blessed realm of love
She sweetly rules and reigns.

You may follow fashion's fancy
But pray you, have the grace
To leave the little, homey house,
And flowery garden-place,
And the window, with the sunshine
Of this dear, remembered face.

You may follow fashion's fancy,
But, I pray you, leave to me
The chair, there in the corner,
Just the way it used to be,
And the dear devoted mother,
With the children at her knee.

No matter how old a mother is,
she watches her middle-aged children
for signs of improvement.
—Florida Scott-Maxwell
The Measure of My Days

I cannot forget my mother.
Though not as sturdy as others,
she is my bridge.
When I needed to get across,
she steadied herself long enough
for me to run across safely.
—Renita Weems

A mother is the truest friend we have,
when trials, heavy and sudden, fall upon us;
when adversity takes the place of prosperity;
when friends who rejoice with us in our sunshine,
desert us when troubles thicken around us,
still will she cling to us,
and endeavor by her kind precepts and counsels
to dissipate the clouds of darkness,
and cause peace to return to our hearts.
—Washington Irving

The Old Homestead

Ah! there it is, that dear old place,
Unchanged through all the years;
How like some sweet, familiar face
My childhood's home appears;
The grand old trees beside the door
Still spread their branches wide;
The river wanders as of yore,
With sweetly murmuring tide;
The distant hills look green and gay,
The flowers are blooming wild,
And everything looks glad to-day,
As when I was a child.

Happy he
With such a mother! faith in womankind
Beats with his blood, and truth in all things high
Comes easy to him.
—Alfred, Lord Tennyson

What could be more astonishing to witness than the growth of her own
children from infant enigmas to their complex and definite,
yet ever-changing selves.
—Elizabeth Cunningham

If a mother respects both herself and her child
from his very first day onward,
she will never need to teach him respect for others.
—Alice Miller

"A PERFECT WOMAN NOBLY PLANNED."

The Mother

Never too tired to hear or heed
The slightest cry of her child's need;
Never impatient in look or work,
By what tender thoughts her heart is stirred.

Through nights of watching and busy days,
Unwearied, she asks no need of praise;
For others spending and being spent,
She finds therein her sweet content.

Though decked in no robes of silken sheen,
In her small domain she walks a queen;
Outshining far the costliest gem.
A spirit meek is her diadem.

Though fortune frown, she is brave of heart,
No selfish thought in her life has part;
Patient and trustful though storms may lower;
A faithful friend in life's darkest hour.

The Jewelry Box

Faith Andrews Bedford

Tonight is our anniversary and my husband is taking me out. I look through my closet and pick out a deep green velvet dress with long sleeves and a high neck. It looks wonderful with my mother's seed pearl necklace and my grandmother's tiny pearl earrings.

As I sit at my dressing table, my daughter, Eleanor, perches beside. She loves to watch me get dressed for special occasions. "Mama," she addresses my reflection in the mirror, "May I pick out your jewelry?"

"Of course," I reply.

She opens the drawer where I keep my jewelry box and begins to sift through the contents. There are the macaroni necklaces she made me in kindergarten and the locket my husband gave me when we were engaged. In a little box Eleanor finds my old Girl Scout pin and some badges.

She holds several pairs of earrings up to her small ears, then discards them. She tries on several necklaces and shakes her head. At last, with a little cry of delight, she pounces on a pair of long, dangly earrings from

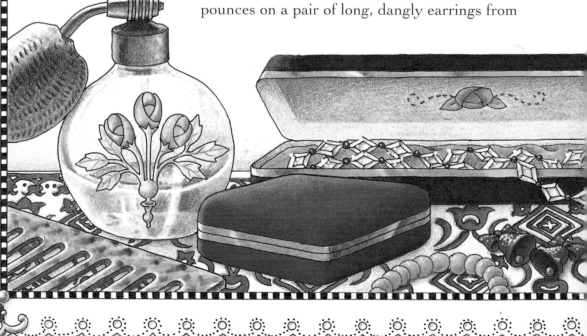

120

Ceylon. They are set with flashing mirrors, obviously left over from the seventies. I wore them with bell bottoms and tunics. In another box she finds two long ropes of beads from the same era.

She drapes the beads around my neck and hands me the earrings. I put them on and give my head a little shake. The earrings glitter brightly.

"Perfect!" She sighs with pleasure. We grin at each other in the mirror.

As Eleanor twirls out of the room to tell her father that I am almost ready, I remember how, when I was Eleanor's age, I used to watch, entranced, as my own Mother prepared for an evening out.

While she pinned up her French twist, I would ask her to tell me where each piece had come from.

In a velvet case lay a beautiful garnet necklace and matching ear rings. Mother told me they belonged to her grandmother who wore them to Boston, where she had seen the famous Sarah Bernhardt perform.

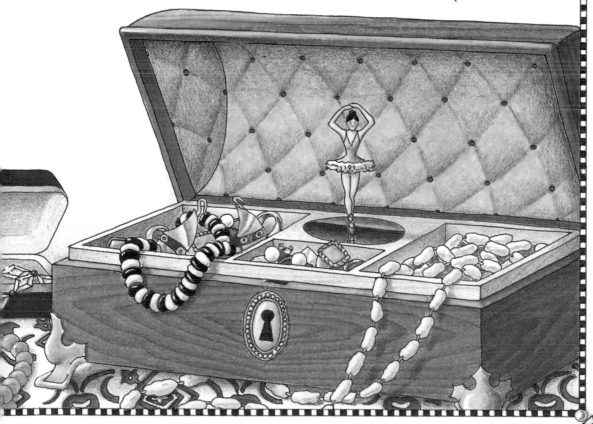

The seed pearl necklace had been given to Mother by her god-mother as a wedding present. Like me, she always wore it with the tiny pearl earrings her grandmother left her. Now I have inherited both.

My favorite things in the drawer were the gifts my Father had given her. In a velvet box was a necklace of rhinestones that glittered with the brilliance of real diamonds. Mother told me they were not diamonds at all, but I thought she still looked just like a princess.

When Father went on a business trip to Arizona, he brought Mother back a ring with a big square of turquoise. It just fit her ring finger; it was too big for my thumb.

For her fortieth birthday, he presented her with some earrings from India. The black enamel had been cut away to reveal silver figures of dancing women bent into impossible positions. My sisters and I tried to imitate them. We couldn't.

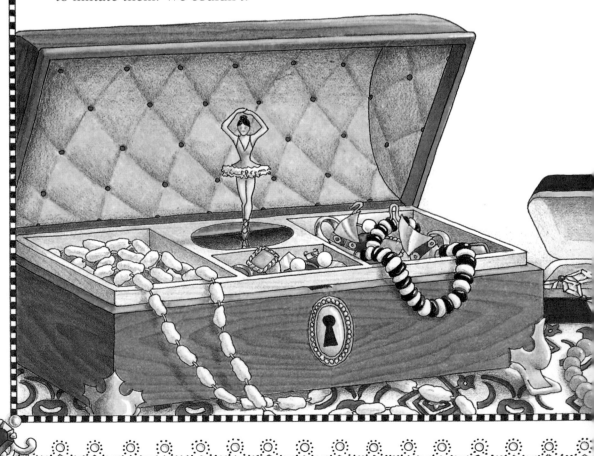

The Christmas I was ten I had saved up enough money to buy Mother some earrings at the five and dime: two red plastic bells hung from tiny bows. The edges had been sprinkled with silver glitter. Mother wore them all Christmas day. She shook her head frequently to show us how they actually made a little tinkling sound.

A few days later, I came into her room just in time to help zip up her black and white taffeta evening dress.

"Will you pick out some earrings for me, dear?" she asked.

Opening her drawer I sorted through the options. Her dress was pretty, I thought, but it needed a bit of color. I proudly pulled out the little red plastic bells.

"Just the thing," she said, putting them on. I looked at her and thought no one ever was more beautiful.

My husband's voice pulls me back to the present. "Ready?" he asks.

"Almost," I reply, putting Mother's pearls and Grandmother's earrings back into my jewelry box.

As I come down the stairs, my beads swinging and the brass earrings flashing in the light, I look down and see Eleanor's proud face. "You look beautiful," she sighs.

"Only with your help," I reply as I kiss her good night. She will be asleep by the time I return.

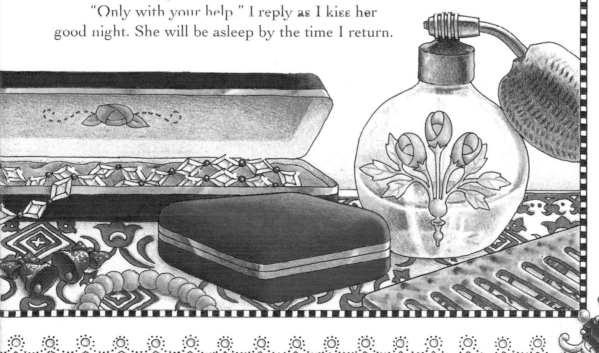

Home Again
Abbie C. McKeever

Home again; mother, your boy will remain
For a time, at least, in the old home again.
How good to see you in your cornered nook
With knitting, or sewing, or paper, or book;
The same sweet mother my boyhood knew,
The faithful, the patient, the tender, and true.

You have changed; ah, well, maybe
A few gray hairs in the brown I see;
A mark or two under smiling eyes,
So lovingly bent in your glad surprise;
'Tis I who have changed; ah, mother mine,
From a teasing lad to manhood's prime.

No longer I climb on your knee at night
For a story told in the soft firelight;
No broken slate, or book all torn,
Do I bring to you with its edges worn;
But I'll come to you with my graver cares;
You'll help me bear them with tender prayers.

I'll come again as of old, and you
Will help the man to be brave and true;
For the man's the boy, only older grown,
And the world has many a stumbling-stone.
Ah, mother mine, there is always rest
When I find you in the home nest.

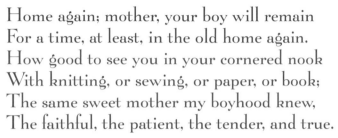

Braided Lives
Marge Piercy

Now that I am in my forties, she tells me I'm beautiful; now that I am in my forties, she sends me presents and we have the long, personal and even remarkably honest phone calls I always wanted so intensely I forbade myself to imagine them. How strange. Perhaps Shaw was correct and if we lived to be several hundred years old, we would finally work it all out. I am deeply grateful. With my poems, I finally won even my mother.
The longest wooing of my life.

Acknowledgments

The publisher gratefully acknowledges permission to reprint the following:

page 11, "Mother O' Mine" by Jan Miller Girando. Copyright © 1993 by Mary Engelbreit Ink.

page 19, "Mother's Song," author unknown, reprinted by permission from Terry Kluytmans's website www.kididdles.com.

pages 24-25, "What Mama Saw" written by Emilie Poulsson, adapted by Terry Kluytmans for www.kididdles.com. Copyright © 1999 Terry Kluytmans. Reprinted by permission.

page 45, "Mama's Lullaby" written by Grace Hall, adapted by Terry Kluytmans for www.kididdles.com. Copyright © 1998 Terry Kluytmans. Reprinted by permission.

pages 60-61, "My Two Sons" copyright © by Melody Carlson. Reprinted by permission.

page 63, "My Daughter" by Jessie Wilmore Murton from *Whatsoever Things Are Lovely* by Jessie Wilmore Murton, copyright © 1948 by Review and Herald Publishing Association. Reprinted with permission.

pages 64-65, "When You Thought I Wasn't Looking" by Mary Rita Schilke Korzan, a poem inspired by the author's mother, Blanche Elizabeth Montgomery Schilke. Copyright © 1980 Mary Rita Schilke Korzan. Reprinted with permission from the author.

pages 70-73, "A Pinch of This and a Pinch of That," author unknown, first appeared in *Ideals* magazine.

page 74, "The Watcher" by Margaret Widdemer from Cross Currents, copyright © 1921 by Harcourt, Brace and Company, Inc.

page 76-81, "The Cap that Mother Made" a Swedish tale from *Up One Pair of Stairs of My Bookhouse,* copyright © 1920, 1925. Edited by Olive Beaupré Miller.

page 98, "Baby Shoes" by Isla Paschal Richardson. Copyright © Branden Publishing Co. Reprinted with permission.

page 109, "Honoring the Great Mother" excerpt from *Simple Abundance* by Sarah Ban Breathnach. Copyright © 1995 by Sarah Ban Breathnach. Reprinted by permission of Warner Books, Inc.

page 120-121, "The Jewelry Box" by Faith Andrews Bedford first appeared in *Mary Engelbreit's Home Companion* magazine, copyright © 1998 by Faith Andrews Bedford. Reprinted by permission of the author.

The publisher also wishes to acknowledge the contributions of the following people for their research and cooperation in providing material for this book.

Eunice Anderson for contributing the following pieces: "Motherhood" by Hilda Ford Sherman, page 17; "Love at First Sight" by Francis Woodworth Howells, page 18; "A Sisterhood Apart" by Nina Stiles, pages 27; and "Mother, Now I Understand" by Virginia Safford Jackson, page 101.

Penny Parker, at http://members.aol.com/mempenny/mothers.html., for the following: "A Mother Is . . . ," page 87; "What Do Mothers Do All Day," page 92; and "Where Does Mom Keep Her Memories?," page 94.

Andrews McMeel Publishing has made every effort to contact the copyright holders.

Author Index

Title Index

POETRY

PROSE

SONGS

Credits

Any book that comes into this world is the result of care and attention of a large group of people. Special thanks to the following, who worked so hard to make this book possible:

Jackie Alhstrom
Eunice Anderson
David Arnold
Stephanie Barken
Pam Dobek
Michelle Dorenkamp
Stephanie Farley
Ann Feldmann
Wende Fink
Erin Friedrich
Casey Frisch
Becky Kanning
Jean Lowe
Elizabeth Nuelle
Marti Petty
Patrick Regan
Jennifer Schoeneberg
Christine Wilkison

To everyone at Mary Engelbreit Studios and Andrews McMeel Publishing, my heartfelt thanks for making this book a reality.

The End